PRAYERS FOR IMPOSSIBLE DAYS

Paul Geres

PRAYERS FOR
IMPOSSIBLE DAYS

Translated by Ingalill H. Hjelm

First published in 1976 by
Fortress Press
Box 1209
Minneapolis
MN55440
USA

First published in Great Britain in 1976 by
Society for Promoting Christian Knowledge
Holy Trinity Church
Marylebone Road
London NW1 4DU

Fourth impression 2003

British Library Cataloguing-in-Publication Data

A catalogue record for this book is available from the British Library

ISBN 0-281-02954-7

Printed in Great Britain by Bookmarque Ltd, Croydon, Surrey

CONTENTS

We all know that there are impossible days. There
are days when suffering seems to drain us of everything. Everything except our knowledge that it,
suffering, is there. Time itself even seems to become
identical with pain.

On such days it is hard to meet friends, even our
closest friends. A visit, a job, life goes on. Everything
seems to be like a mirror which reflects the unbearable
light of the pain inside us. Whether the pain is of
the heart or of the body is of little importance.
Either way, the pain is still the same. There are,
indeed, impossible days.

There are also days, less difficult, when we are simply
tired of everything. It is not as if we were suffering
from anything specific. Things are usually not that
clear. It is life itself which weighs us down, because
every day seems to be like the one before, and each
morning brings the same wear and tear as it has for
five, six, or ten years. And finally this begins to add
up, and the burden becomes heavy.

And try to pray under these circumstances! When
we want only one thing — to hurt less, change our

lives, get away from other people and especially from ourselves.

Yet precisely on those days ought we to pray. To pray, to step back from ourselves, to turn to this mysterious God who seems always to sear us because we neither see him face to face nor see the decisive light which he casts over our human existence.

But is wanting to pray enough? It is of little help to know that the grace to pray is ours. There are still impossible days when we desire no consolation, even that of asking for consolation.

It is in order to help my friends, known and unknown, that I have written these prayers. They come from many encounters with suffering and pain. Their value — if any — is that they reflect many confidences given to me and faithfully recall the secret lives and daily struggles of many individuals crushed by impossible days. It goes without saying that they are not meant to replace personal prayer; that is of course out of the question. They are here simply as a help, in case they should be needed, and as such, I offer them.

1 PRAYER TO ADMIT MISTAKES

O my God, how hard it is to have made a mistake . . .

Simply to accept it, without looking for excuses.
Without trying to escape the burden of the mistake,
without making two or three others pay the conse-
quences, or blaming it on society, circumstances, or
just bad luck. Without trying to find ten good
reasons . . .

How difficult it is to accept a mistake . . .

Without being angry and defending myself with
meaningless arguments. Without always attempting
to be blameless, free of sin . . .

O God, set me free from the fear of having to admit
to my mistakes. Whether mistakes at work, at school,
or at home.

'Let what you say be simply "Yes" or "No" '
(Matt. 5.37).

In order to do this, Lord, you have to be an adult.
An adult, and not a tight-lipped little boy or girl with
a bad conscience.

1

'When I was a child, I spoke like a child, I thought like a child, I reasoned like a child; when I became a man, I gave up my childish ways' (1 Cor. 13.11).

Lord, in order that I may accept the healing bite of truth, set me free from myself.

2 PRAYER FOR DAYS WHEN
YOU ARE TIRED OF OTHERS

Lord, how they tire me out. How they tire me out, people whom you have asked me to call my brothers and sisters.

My brothers and sisters . . . They aren't always fun. But they are always *different*. And that's the worst thing of all.

All of them are different, and they all impose on me something special, something peculiar which confuses or hurts me.

Each of them forces me to admit to something. And it's not so easy to admit that they are *different*.

Each of them forces me to understand something. I don't always feel like it, Lord. It becomes very tiring.

Each of them forces me to love something. To accept something the way it is. Even if I find it painful, embarrassing, unreasonable.

God, it's tiring to love other people. Sometimes I have such a great desire to lock myself up within the narrow circle of friends whom I understand without difficulty, whom I know intimately, and whose presence always gives me the same warmth, the same peace — I was about to say the same comfort!

Lord, help me never to close myself to others. Help me never to say 'I don't understand you' as I turn my back to return in peace and quiet to my own home where there is no room for them.

Help me never to put labels on anyone, saying 'he is such and such'. O Lord, keep me from putting them in pigeonholes.

Help me rather to find on the face of each one of them the traits of the children they once were. Then, and then alone, O Lord, shall I understand.

3 PRAYER FOR DAYS WHEN THINGS GO AGAINST YOU

Everything went wrong today, Lord. It all happened at once. Someone else got the job that I was so well qualified for. I had counted on the support of my friend, but he happened to be ill. Why did he have to fall sick just today? And then I got a migraine headache. That was more than I could take. Later, I had to walk home in the rain, and I got soaked to the bone.

So I'm terribly angry, Lord. Pray to you . . . I'm afraid that I'll tell you the same stupid things I did as a child when it rained one Saturday. A day of holiday — just the day when I didn't want it to rain. It's ludicrous: just a while ago, when I learned that my friend was ill, I sensed the same frustrated anger that a disappointed child feels. And for this I must ask your forgiveness.

Basically I reason like a child. At my age . . . Yes, it's true. I think I can see through your schemes. Mean, devious schemes. Yours, my God. I imagine that I know your thoughts just as I think I know those of my superiors. But what do I really know about them? It's hard enough to understand the thoughts of people you have lived with all your life.

I so easily become unfair, Lord, on days when things
go against me. I need somebody who can take over
the responsibility, somebody on whom I can vent
my anger. I almost begin to wonder what I've done
to you for everything to go so wrong. As if you had
whims and fancies like mine!

Yes, God, everything went wrong today, and it wasn't
my fault, and I was about to think that it was yours
and that you did a poor job in creating the world.
Always this incurable habit of re-ordering the universe
so that it suits me.

'The eye is the lamp of the body. So, if your eye is
sound . . .' (Matt. 6.22).

Lord, give me the gift to see the world as it is. Even
when I have failed to make use of an opportunity
which will not soon come back again. Even when I
have a headache on the same day that I have something very important to do. Even when I get soaked
in the rain.

Lord, give me the gift to see the truth. And also a
sense of humour.

4   A BITTER PERSON'S PRAYER

I know, Lord, that my future lies behind me. Since
yesterday, I've known that my situation will never
improve. I needed so many things to succeed: fame
and the right contacts. But I thought honesty was
enough.

I admit that it makes me feel ill at ease, Lord, to see
younger persons promoted, all the young ones who
know the art of climbing. They'll succeed. As far as
my position is concerned, it will remain the same.

I've begun to hate people who pass me by. Of course
they haven't done a thing to hurt me. They have
simply been lucky. And that's reason enough for me
to hate them. Where were they when the war was
fought? They were studying in peace and quiet and
passing their final exams. But where was I . . .?

I never had a break to begin with. At least that's what
I'm tempted to think. Why did I set my goals so high?
Another trick of the imagination. When you are
young, you believe so much in the future . . . Every
hope is permissible. Everything must turn out for the
best. Later on you discover that others are there too.

Lord, I want you to help me. Help me grow old with
greater calm and dignity. Grow old without bitterness.

Nothing was promised to me. Nobody owed me anything. I must tell myself this over and over again.
When you are young, it's so easy to think that life
owes you everything: the present, the future, a
career . . . And then, as the years pass by, you discover that this was nothing but a dream. Fiction.

It's sheer grace to realize this. Grace for which I
must thank you. So many people hold you responsible
for their unrealized dreams . . . Lord, let me
never make you responsible for mine. In fact, Lord,
did you yourself have a 'great career'?

5   PRAYER AFTER A SEPARATION

This time yesterday, we were still together. It's harder now. Harder than at the moment when we left each other.

I feel desolate tonight, Lord, and so alone. I feel the pain slowly awakening, as when you come out of anaesthesia, and I knew that it would be like this.

You never realize right away what happens. It's not until about a day later that you begin to understand.

I don't know what else to tell you, Lord, except that I'm suffering. This time yesterday . . .

The closer we got to parting, the more I felt that the roughest part of it all would be today. To continue to live when you have absolutely no desire or joy left, when nothing matters any longer. On the train, I said to myself that from now on nothing was going to hurt me. Nothing was going to make me suffer again.

I wished so deeply that I would never get attached to anyone again, so that I would not have to suffer any more. I said to myself: 'This has got to be the last time.'

Lord, if only people could stop holding on to me.

Since I always lose them. Since nothing lasts. Since absolutely nothing lasts forever. After this last relationship, I promised myself to stop loving.

And now, Lord, I begin to wonder if it's right to think that way.

To withdraw from others to avoid suffering at all costs . . . That would obviously be one 'solution'. Not at all original, as old as the wisdom of antiquity and as old as the heart's revolt against the pain of loss.

This wisdom leads to too much disappointment and agony. It isn't as true and pure and simple as your gospel.

As for the rest, Lord, tonight I'd better work, try to find some distraction, and try to get to sleep.

Tomorrow is another day.

6 PRAYER AFTER SEEING A CHILD DIE

I have just come back from the hospital. The nurse gave me no hope. Any moment now.

Lord, I don't understand. And yet I know there is nothing to understand and nothing to do.

Just to be there, and pray as best I can. I went into her room, as I had done every night for the last eight weeks. Today, for the first time, she didn't recognize me.

She looked as if she were very far away. Far from me, far from the hospital, from everything.

Sixteen years old . . .

I looked at her things on the chair, at her slippers by the bed, as if . . . I looked at clothes which she would never put on again. Lord, I ask you, what could she have done to suffer so much and to die at sixteen?

And then I realized the enormity of what I was going to say. As if events of this kind — the death of a sixteen-year-old girl — could be solved like a problem in geometry. As if I could reason this through like once — a long time ago in school — I calculated the speed of a train.

What do I know, my God, about the fate of man? About life and death? I am not forty yet.

What do I know of the mystery of this child? Of your love for her?

What do I know about anything, except that you exist?

7 PRAYER WHEN LIFE
HAS BECOME ROUTINE

Lord, when I woke up this morning, I said to myself
that this would be a day just like every other day.

And it was.

I took the same tube train as every morning, I read
the same comments in the paper on an international
situation which never changes.

I went up the same staircase as usual, and on my desk
I found the same piles of papers to go through —
papers which have been exactly the same for almost
ten years.

The porter was the same and so was the supervisor.
They looked just as they usually do; they had that
blank expression which says that nothing new is going
to happen today.

For lunch I had the same old thing to eat. It was
Monday. I went back to my desk until five o'clock.
And then I just came home, knowing full well that
tomorrow it will start all over again.

God, I'm tired of it all.

I had hoped for something completely different. I had dreamed that some day I would lead an active and exciting life. That was a dream. Yet it can be painful to wake up from a dream.

I'll never be anything but what I am.

I know that some people would be happy in my situation. True. But that doesn't help my fatigue and boredom.

Lord, let me talk to you tonight about my fatigue, about my desire to get away from here. To whom can I speak about this, if not to you?

Nobody understands. They say: 'What is he complaining about?' And perhaps they are right. It's only normal that you do your job.

Therefore I shall talk about it only with you.

Don't change anything. My life doesn't have to change. I must change.

Lord, help me to think less about myself.

Help me to see that there are other people besides myself. For whom today is just like every other day.

8 PRAYER FOR SOMEONE WHO HAS GROWN TIRED OF THE CHURCH

Lord, nothing has worked out the way I thought it would.

People in your Church disappoint me. I've wondered many times if I shouldn't give them up and come to terms with you alone. Their shortcomings hurt and upset me. This failure to live what they preach offends me, especially since they claim to represent what is right. This self-assurance also . . . When you hear some of them, you might conclude that you personally exemplify the truth of their every word. Even when they speak of things they don't know anything about.

I wish they were more saintly. I wish they were more humble. Quite frankly, Lord, they make me angry at times. I think that you were almost bordering on carelessness when you said to the disciples: 'He who hears you hears me' (Luke 10.16).

And yet, Lord, I mustn't turn my back on your Church. I mustn't separate myself from the whole under the pretence that I would find you more easily then. I want to stay among your own, where you are.

When all is said and done, you have supported and upheld us all. I must learn to love. Not a sentimental love. That's not what you ask for. What you want is love which knows no aversions. Lord, I should like to pledge to you my effort to love. But I need your help.

Make me understand that my brothers and sisters are human. Like me, no worse and no better. How else could you have revealed yourself to man except through man?

What did I expect? That your people would be perfect? Did I forget the history and nature of man, and what salvation is all about, when I dreamed of a Church free from misery, human ambitions, and failure?

I had built my own dream Church . . . a Church that was not human, didn't even exist. Is your Church responsible for my dreams? Can it be blamed for my expectations? Lord, let me not forget the human condition.

Lord, guard me against my optimism as well as my pessimism. Teach me to be just, which is something quite different — and infinitely more difficult.

'No one will take your joy from you' (John 16.22).

16

9   PRAYER OF A DISCOURAGED BOSS

Lord, a long time ago — a very long time ago — I
wanted to make my employees my friends. I would
have liked never to punish, never to blame. I even
thought that with a little bit of luck I might never
have to say anything offensive. To be like that I
thought it sufficient to know 'the tricks', and I was
convinced that I knew them.

I had just forgotten human nature — mine as well
as theirs.

There really are people you cannot change. When
someone used to tell me that, I smiled: 'What a
pessimistic attitude! I am certainly going to change
all that . . .' I have changed nothing. There actually
are people whom you cannot change or do anything
with. People whom it is difficult to be with, no
matter how good your intentions are. 'O faithless and
perverse generation, how long am I to be with you
and bear with you?' (Luke 9.41).

Lord, the first thing that I have to learn from you is
to accept them as they are.

Admit that there is nothing attractive about them and
yet count myself responsible for their happiness.

17

Admit that they have neither intelligence nor judgment and yet not cease to respect them. Admit that they always feel slighted, that they are always suspicious. Even though I have done everything I can do to be fair.

Never to tell myself that they don't deserve any better.

Lord, I wanted to be loved . . . Or rather, I wanted to charm them. I wanted to play the young boss who is loved by his employees. That was a fiction, Lord, and a bad one at that. First of all, Lord, forgive me for having wanted to charm them. And then simply help me to work for them.

10 PRAYER AFTER A FAMILY BREAK-UP

Lord, why must I relive all this again tonight? The family I no longer have, our battles, and our final break-up. It's ancient history.

It's been so long since we broke up. Since I left never to come back again.

The desire to live together again is dead now, dead at both ends. The chasm is too wide for any goodwill to bridge it.

When you leave one another after an argument, after a violent scene, there is still some hope. But when we left one another, there had been no argument. What good was arguing? Love was dead. Together we had put an end to its drawn-out agony. The agony of twenty years, the result of our incurable stupidity. Twenty years of small wounds which passed by unnoticed. Misunderstandings which we thought were unimportant but were of deadly importance to love.

Lord, it's too late. We're too far from each other now. And the habit has taken root, the sad habit of never seeing one another again.

An attempt at reconciliation would only make us relive our suffering. You cannot undo what has once been done; it was before it happened that we should have been more thoughtful. When there was still time to love.

There are instances, Lord, and you know that, when love demands silence.

We must wait patiently until you set things right, no doubt beyond this world. Here everything is estranged even though we forgive one another. One ought never to hate. There is so little time to love.

Help all of us, Lord, not to confuse resignation with indifference. To have the courage to carry the burden of our regret that we never loved enough.

11 PRAYER WHEN YOU
WORRY ABOUT MONEY

Lord, I have just balanced my cheque book. And
now I must turn to you to find calm and peace. And
dignity as well.

This dignity which has been eroded for twenty years
because of the awful worry about 'making ends meet'.

This peace which I'm deprived of for fear of not
getting through another month. This calm which I
lose when my small income disappears and I never
have a penny left.

What I fear, Lord, is not really poverty. I'll survive
one way or another.

What I'm afraid of is degradation. Afraid of no longer
thinking of anything but money, just because I don't
have any.

Afraid of always making easy comparisons with
others who earn more. And this a hundred times a
day, in front of shop windows and at the counters
of department-stores.

Lord, I'm also afraid of jealousy. Afraid of saying, with a scornful grin: 'Some people are just lucky . . .' Afraid of hatred also.

And to top it all off, Lord, I've discovered that I'm getting greedy.

That's why I'm talking to you, Lord. To ask you for the grace to let me keep my dignity.

12 PRAYER ON ENTERING HOSPITAL

Lord, this is a gloomy place. It's not worse than I had
imagined, but it's different. It's not like anything
else I've known. And that's what's confusing.

So I'm afraid. That's all.

The ambulance, the stretcher, the lift. Everything
went so fast. I wanted to tell everybody: 'There must
be a mistake. This can't be me . . .' And yet it is me.

I should like to know, Lord, know for certain . . .
Just a minute ago, a young man in a white coat came
in. He had the face of a young boy, but his manner was
confident. His eyes were sharp and penetrating. And
completely impersonal. I can hardly remember what
he said to me. Something like: 'Well, we'll see . . .'
And then he said something to the nurse as he left.

At any rate, I don't know anything more than I did
before.

And that's what I can't bear. It makes me afraid. Not
to know.

Not to know what exactly is wrong with me, nor

what they can do for me, nor how long they will keep me here.

To be dependent. To realize that I am dependent on a great many things and a great many people.

I should like to ask you a favour, Lord.

Peace? Yes, I certainly need that. But there's more. I need much more — for I don't know how this will end.

I would ask that you give me the greatest gift a sick person can have — yes, to be joyful.

13 PRAYER WHEN YOU ARE
TIRED OF PRAYING

Lord, I don't want to pray tonight. I'm too frighten-
ed; I don't want to take the risk of listening to you.
That would require another effort — always another
effort. And I don't want to do that tonight.

These long days, when nothing surprising happens,
bore me . . . All of these days pass by, and I don't
even know if I have made any progress, if I have
improved at all.

It is dark, and soon there will be another day. And
when I wake up   if I manage to fall asleep — I know
that I'll not have changed. I'll be the same. No better,
no worse, the same daily tasks ahead of me, the same
opportunities to do something good — which I always
fail to recognize.

And yet, how many times haven't I asked you for
perfection? 'Be perfect as your heavenly Father is
perfect.' I am a failure.

And now that I'm getting older, I wonder if I will
ever succeed . . . and if it's even worth trying.

I wonder, Lord, if I've sought perfection honestly enough. I should have liked to dress up in it, be beautiful . . . To be a saint to others and to myself . . . I must really refrain from this and admit, quite simply, once and for all, that I am only who I am.

Maybe, Lord, this is really what you mean by 'becoming like little children'. To accept myself with the same openness of heart with which you have accepted us all — just as we are.

Simply to accept that I'm one of those to whom you came: the sinners to whom your gospel is so kind. I must admit that your preference for sinners used to annoy me. Your preference for everything that falls to the ground, for everything that 'isn't worth much'.

Once I would have defended the Pharisees. I would even have found good reasons for it. Now it's different.

Now it's the others that I understand, all those with whom the gospel is concerned. The poor and the average human beings who know that they don't amount to much. No doubt I'm beginning to understand . . . that I too am one of those.

And that it was *for us* that you came.

But, Lord, don't demand too much from me tonight.

14 PRAYER TO BEAR INGRATITUDE

Lord, I would never have believed that about my
'friend'. If anyone else had done it, I would have
been hurt. But my 'friend'? I am crushed. After all
I've done for him.

My first reaction was indignation. Lord, forgive me
one thing which is certainly not to my credit. When
I saw how he acted, I immediately thought: 'Just
wait until I can show him, then he'll learn . . .' But
what would he have 'learned'?

I am the one who has much to learn. For one thing:
that people are what they are. It is said that you
'knew what was in man' (John 2.25). You knew
what was in us, yet in spite of everything you never
turned your.back on us. And for another thing: that
not everybody can be grateful. And that this is not
always their fault. At any rate it isn't your fault.

The hardest lesson perhaps is to learn to love them
in spite of everything, to wish them well even when
they betray you or go in whatever direction the wind
blows.

Lord, I claim to know something about life, but I
didn't know. I didn't know that favours are so easily
forgotten.

One more thing, Lord. And this is much harder to
put into words. This morning when I discovered that
my friend had forgotten me, I was on the verge of
comparing myself to you when you suffered and
were betrayed.

O my God, how absurd!

15 PRAYER FOR PATIENCE

I'll never get an answer to my letter. And yet I should have had one by now. I can't stand this uncertainty any longer.

I'm tired of waiting, Lord.

Always waiting. Waiting for the post, waiting to learn the terms of a contract, waiting to recover from illness, waiting in a queue, waiting for the bus. Waiting . . . for everything.

I come to you again, Lord, to ask you for the gift of patience.

But once more I must wait. I should like to think that patience could be had right away.

At least, in that perfect world of my own creation. In my own world, where time never stands still.

Lord, I should like to regain some understanding of nature and its rhythms. To accept that the harvest needs sun. To accept that man needs sleep. To accept that you must think and rest before you answer a question. To accept that it takes nine months for a child to be born. To accept, without complaint, the delays that are part of the nature of things.

To accept, at last, that I live in the world of your creation and not in a world of my own making. I stand to lose nothing on that bargain.

Lord, teach me to love the long and fruitful passing of the days and seasons, and the infinitely slow growth of the fruits . . .

Help me to wait for patience.

16 PRAYER FOR A SINNER
WHO THOUGHT HE HAD CHANGED

Lord, nothing is going right tonight. I didn't think I was capable of this. I thought I had got rid of it. But, no!

This time I really feel like letting go of everything. If this is what it all comes to, I would rather give up at once. For you know, Lord, that I have tried.

What hurts me deep down is that I must give up the habit of thinking so highly of myself.

Lord, I must admit that the thing that bothers me most is my wounded pride.

Lord, I know it isn't good. But I would rather admit it to you directly, without beating about the bush. My regret isn't pure. I do regret my sin.

But what I regret most is myself. The self I thought had changed. The self that I was beginning to feel proud of — like Seneca, I believe it was, who visited his soul every evening and took pleasure in finding it in order.

Forgive me, Lord, for having loved myself more than you. For having put myself before you.

Teach me to bear my sin and not just drag it behind me. Help me to accept with courage that in your eye I am a sinner, and help me not to sulk about it like a little child.

Give me your forgiveness. For my sin. But also . . . for my wounded pride.

Lord, I thank you for having made me realize that I am like all other men, 'extortioners, unjust, adulterers' (Luke 18.11).

Lord, it's hard never to know a moment's peace. Not to be able to do one thing which isn't destroyed by worry.

And not to be able to do anything about it. 'You must pull yourself together . . .' I've been told that a hundred times. If I only could . . .

For want of something better, Lord, I now give you my fears and my worries.

The letters I rewrite three times because something is always missing.

The intense fear of a telephone call when anyone leaves on a journey.

The gas tap which I check and recheck and the front door which I make sure is locked several times every night.

The fear every time I have a headache that it might be something serious.

The worries of each day which I mull over and over

again as soon as I have turned off the light.

Lord, help me at least to do whatever I can to get out of this depressing world of mine.

Protect me from these shadows, which are a hundred times more frightening than the real thing itself.

I need courage, Lord. To resist the insidious need to do the same thing over and over again when I know it was well done the first time. To resist consulting the medical dictionary every time I get a headache.

I need your help, Lord. To gain my freedom from one day to the other. To conquer, no matter how small the victories, my nightmares.

Lord, in my night, I need to hear you say: 'It is I — do not be afraid' (John 6.20).

18   PRAYER AFTER AN EXHAUSTING DAY

Pray to you, Lord? No, I'd rather go to sleep and just have you keep an eye on me. That's enough for tonight.

I don't want to think or even move any longer. I would like to commit myself to you just as I am without any more tossing and turning in your hands like a restless child.

I have more worries tonight than I can bear.

It's late. It's time to sleep.

I ought to have written those letters too. No! Tomorrow.

Lord, teach me to rest. Teach me to leave things be and not to think that I must have everything in order before I go to sleep.

As if I could ever get everything in order.

Teach me to accept my tiredness without getting upset or bitter about it, without complaining about my need for sleep. Teach me to put my papers away without regrets that I can't do everything.

Teach me to finish *one* day. How else will I ever learn to die . . . For there will be work left after I'm gone . . .

Teach me to accept that I'm not you . . .

19 PRAYER WHEN
YOU ARE ALWAYS AILING

Lord, I'm tired of being ill all the time, sick of
minor but exhausting ailments, and sick of feeling
weak after every effort to accomplish something.

I am tired of hearing people say: 'There is always
something wrong with . . .'

True, there *is* always something wrong with me.
Nothing serious, nothing which makes others look
at me and sadly think: 'It could happen to me . . .'

Not even that. What happens to me is of no great
consequence. Minor little illnesses which don't scare
anyone: a headache here and a cold there; then
something wrong with my stomach, and then something else again. Little nothings.

But there is no end to it. And my patience is running
out.

I'm beginning to dream about another life, a life
without illness. A strong and healthy life where I get
up fresh and rested every morning, ready to meet
everything with a smile. A beautiful life: the product
of my imagination.

And then I begin to envy people. The healthy ones. I think it's unjust: their relaxed expression, their fresh complexion, their meals without fears and worries. And that smile they put on when they say to me: 'So, what's wrong with you today?' as if they knew what illness is all about.

Forgive me, Lord, for having been unjust. I know that it isn't altogether my fault. But I was nevertheless angry with them. That's stupid.

Teach me, Lord, to understand — that they don't understand.

When I don't feel like doing a thing, give me strength. Strength not to give in, as they say. Strength to try at any rate.

Lord, help me to bear my endless little miseries with some flair.

20 PRAYER FOR THE
   DARK NIGHT OF FAITH

To pace back and forth in the middle of the night
gets tiring, Lord. To walk without seeing is possible
for a moment, but for long . . .

'Will you also go away?' (John 6.67). Lord, I understand those to whom you said that. And those who
found the words in your message too harsh. Some
preferred to leave.

There are times when I feel like doing that too.

I wish that everything was clear, determined, and
orderly. That there no longer was this circle of
darkness which robs me of my desire to walk
towards your light.

Deep down, what I really want to get away from is
the human condition.

For it is, after all, not only the meaning of your
message which escapes me.

What do I know about the conditions which are

called human, what do I know about the secret laws
of the universe, about the reason for life? What do I
know about the people around me, what do I know
about the hearts of my own friends?

What do I know about myself, about my own face,
about the hidden motives behind so many decisions
which I think I make for the right reasons . . .

And then I get angry with you for not already having
given me eyes capable of seeing you face to face.

But if I knew you in the same way that I know things,
would you then be my God?

Lord, help me to believe that the dark night of faith
never is a punishment which you inflict.

21 PRAYER WHEN YOU FEEL
THAT YOU HAVE FAILED

Lord, I know that I don't amount to much in this
world.

I've failed in my studies, I've tried all sorts of jobs,
at least those which don't require any 'special
skills'. I can't hold down a job for more than six
months.

People talk about me and say: 'There goes a failure.'
In a sense, they are right. And I no longer know if I
set my goals too high or too low when I was young.
It's horrible to feel like a failure. When you discover
it, it's too late.

It didn't always bother me. Now I suffer from being
nothing but a failure. It has crept up on me with age.
And it is doubtless too late for me to become anything but — a failure.

I didn't know that life went by so fast.

It's not so easy to begin all over again. People no
longer take you seriously. It's finished: to them you
are just such-and-such, the failure.

There comes a moment when you no longer can start all over again.

Lord, it is surely too late for me to make anything out of my life.

This is a thing that I must admit calmly and without bitterness. Without putting the blame on society, my parents, or other people in general. That would be too easy. At any rate, Lord, I would like to pull myself together once more.

Not to give up too easily, not to accept that I'll forever be the fifth wheel under the cart. Not to cultivate only my own strange specialty — to be good at nothing.

Lord, I so much want to be good at something. Even though I know that it is quite late now.

O God, if I could only get away: I don't know where.
That doesn't matter.

Leave . . .
Like seeds blown by the wind. Escape discipline and
duty, restrictions, everything that limits and crushes
me and forces me to give up what I used to love.

O Lord, I have this yearning for independence again,
the same yearning which I felt when I was fifteen but
which I thought was dead by now. A longing for
adventure and an unquenchable desire for open
horizons. I want to be my own master, not to obey
anyone. I want to tell myself, as so many others do,
that there is no longer any law — simply because I
don't want to have anything to do with one.

But I'm not fifteen years old any more, Lord, and I
know that. And I need your help to realize that
dreams are empty, that life is serious, that there are
other human beings, and that there is work to be
done.

O Lord, help me to face reality, help me to see
clearly, give me that single-minded will which can

aid me whenever I want to give up the problem of the human condition in order to follow my own dreams. On those days, Lord, prevent me from doing foolish things — I've had enough of that. Remind me of the good which is yet to be done, the help yet to be given to some, peace to others.

If I rebel for an instant, God, forgive me, for you know that I desire only to do what you want me to do.

'What do you think? A man had two sons; and he went to the first and said, "Son, go and work in the vineyard today". And he answered, "I will not"; but afterward he repented and went. And he went to the second and said the same; and he answered, "I go, sir," but did not go. Which of the two did the will of his father?' (Matt. 21.28-31).

23   PRAYER TO ACCEPT YOURSELF

When I was a child, Lord, I didn't know. I didn't
know that you can be tired, tired of yourself, and
that you can feel that you have missed out on life.

I've known many temptations, but these are the
worst: to wish for better health, higher intelligence,
a stronger body, a better education. Another job and
some of the appreciation shown to others.

To see others have countless opportunities which I
should have liked and advantages I never had. To
know that it is high time to live and too late to
dream. To know that the impossible will never
happen.

To know this, Lord, is to have a guiding light. The
dreams are over. What is left now is my life — the
real life which I must love! My life such as it is, my
poor health, my poor job, and all the rest I never
wanted.

I should like to accept all this, Lord. And accept
myself, as poor as I am. Help me no longer to
torment myself with thoughts of what 'might have
been', but to find happiness in doing what I can.

For a long time, Lord, I thought that to be free
meant that I could do just about anything. Anything
that occurred to me or that I felt like doing. The
wildest things.

You know that I've wanted to taste all the fruits —
and not always the best.

I've wanted to taste everything in this world. I've
wanted to live everything. To have to choose was just
what I didn't want to do. Should I die, at my age,
without having exhausted everything the world has
to offer?

For a long time, Lord, I believed this, that freedom
meant I could do just about anything. And there are
times when I still do. And I suffer because I can't
experience everything.

Now, Lord, I wish that you would teach me what
true freedom really means. I want to understand at
long last the true meaning of life. But first, I need
the eyes I had as a child.

I need to see, deep down in myself, something pure

which speaks about you, something which remains unchanged, in spite of my poor choices.

I should like to discover in my past the eternal Face which watched over my life when I was a child. 'The Lord is in his place, and I did not know it' (Gen. 16.28).

I now know, Lord, what it means to be free. It means to desire what you desire, to love what you love. And if there has to be a choice, it simply means that I take what you choose.

To be free means to try to find out your purpose for my life, your plans, and your opinions, and to make my own face more like yours. For I was made in your image.

25 PRAYER WHEN YOU
ARE TIRED OF WAR

O Lord, I get depressed by this world of people who act like animals, who cannot rest until they have killed off their prey. Nations which think of nothing but hatred, murder, and massacre bring me close to despair. And I feel like giving up my faith in man, life, in — O Lord, what was I about to say? I want to shout out my disdain for this world, but no, I must not do that.

No, I must resist the despair which overcomes me, and I must not run away.

I must not flee to some ivory tower, far from men and their inhumanity, in order to escape this unbearable world.

I shall remain here, in the midst of this world, in this world as it is, in this world of violence. I shall remain at my post.

Of course I don't amount to much. In the midst of chaos, what does the light of only one soul mean, a faint light which darkness will extinguish? And yet, my God, I must do what I am called to do.

'And what shall I say? "Father, save me from this hour"? No, for this purpose I have come to this hour ... to bear witness to the truth' (John 12.27; 18.37).

I must witness.

To tell — and to show — to all men that there is something other than the darkness, something other than the screams of fear, something other than the meaningless fighting, the ravings of demagogues, and the invasions.

Something other than the tons of scrap iron which are used to kill and the blown-up bridges which then have to be rebuilt. Something other than the immeasurable stupidity of the hordes of people pushing forward — using all the instruments of technological warfare.

Something other than economic control and ideology.

Witness, O my God, to your presence in the midst of this world and reveal to man, in spite of everything and no matter what the cost, the *other* meaning to life.

And when none of these prayers has been of any
comfort to you, then shall you say:

Our Father, who art in heaven,
hallowed be thy name;
thy kingdom come;
thy will be done;
on earth as it is in heaven.
Give us this day our daily bread;
And forgive us our trespasses,
as we forgive those who trespass against us;
And lead us not into temptation,
But deliver us from evil.
For thine is the kingdom, the power, and the glory,
for ever and ever.

Amen.